TIM JEFFS ART
Animal Sketches
Birds

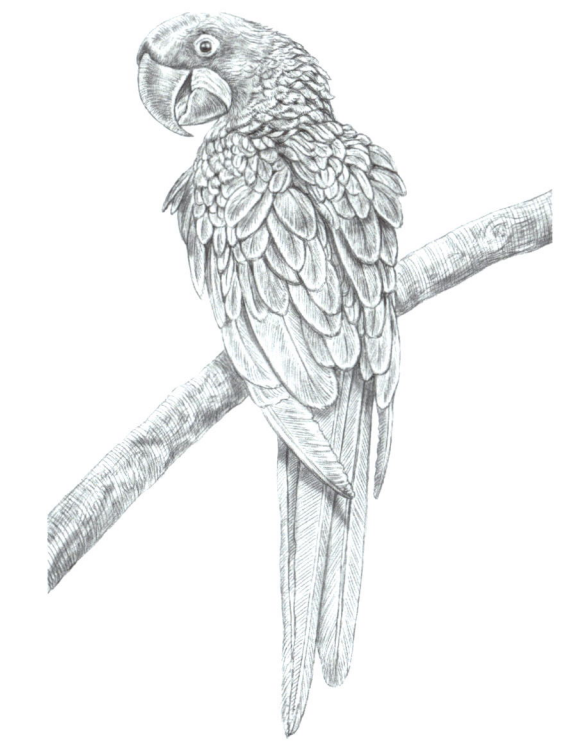

A Special Edition Coloring Book

For Jane, Jenna and Harrison

Dedicated to all of the wonderful colorists who have supported my art and made my drawings more beautiful with their colors, and all the precious creatures that we live among.
A special thank you to Jo Warren for all of her continued support.

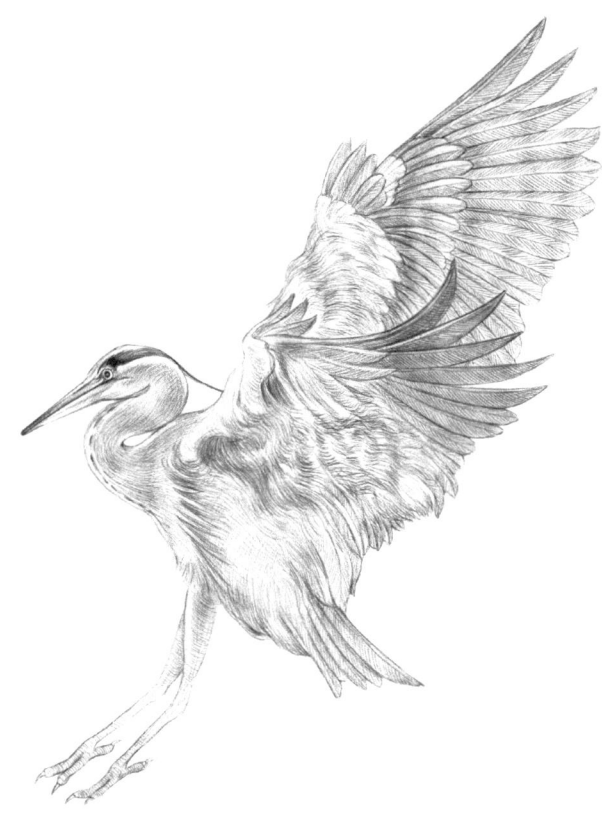

© Copyright 2021 Tim Jeffs Art
All rights reserved. No part of this publication may be reproduced or distributed in any form without the prior written permission of Tim Jeffs Art.

Tim Jeffs Art
376 East Madison Avenue, Dumont, NJ 07628

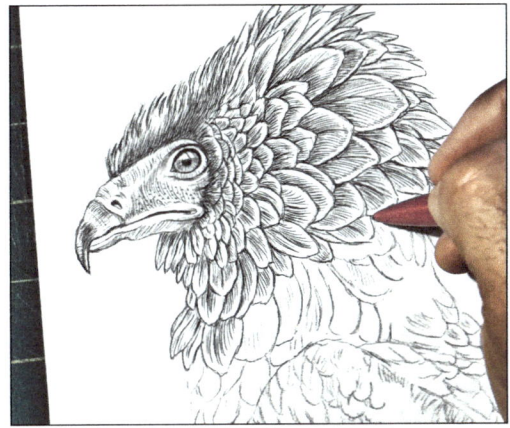 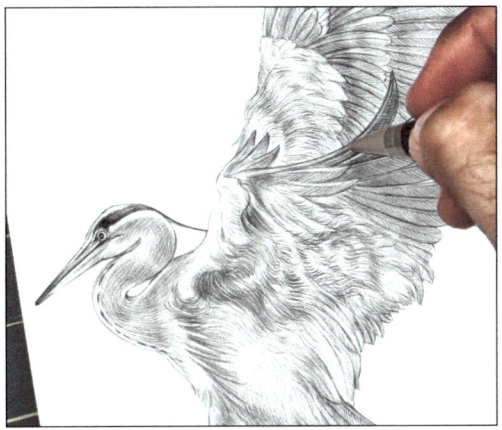 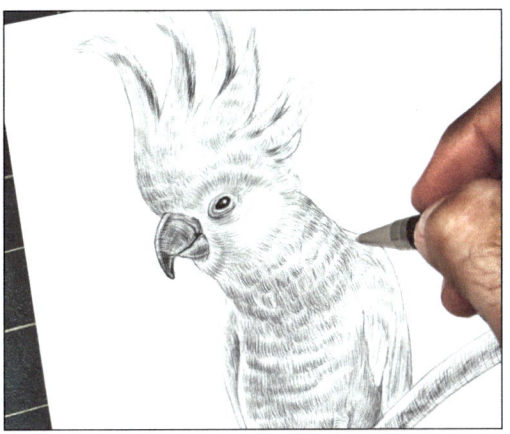

Sketchbook Thoughts

An artist's sketchbook is like a close friend, always nearby and ready to take in whatever is on your mind. It's a place to experiment, explore, and inspire ideas. Most artists will tell you they go nowhere without one, and it's as if you forgot your wallet if you left your sketchbook behind. This book is a collection of 15 black and white ink drawings of birds from my sketchbook. Many of the these drawings are studies of the more involved and complex projects I create, but in certain ways the drawings from my sketchbook have a life that only they can express. I hope you enjoy coloring these animal sketches as much as I enjoyed drawing them, and I know that with your colors, you will bring them to life! Have fun!

GRAYSCALE COLORING LESSON
Great Blue Heron

lesson level: Easy

Coloring the
Great Blue Heron

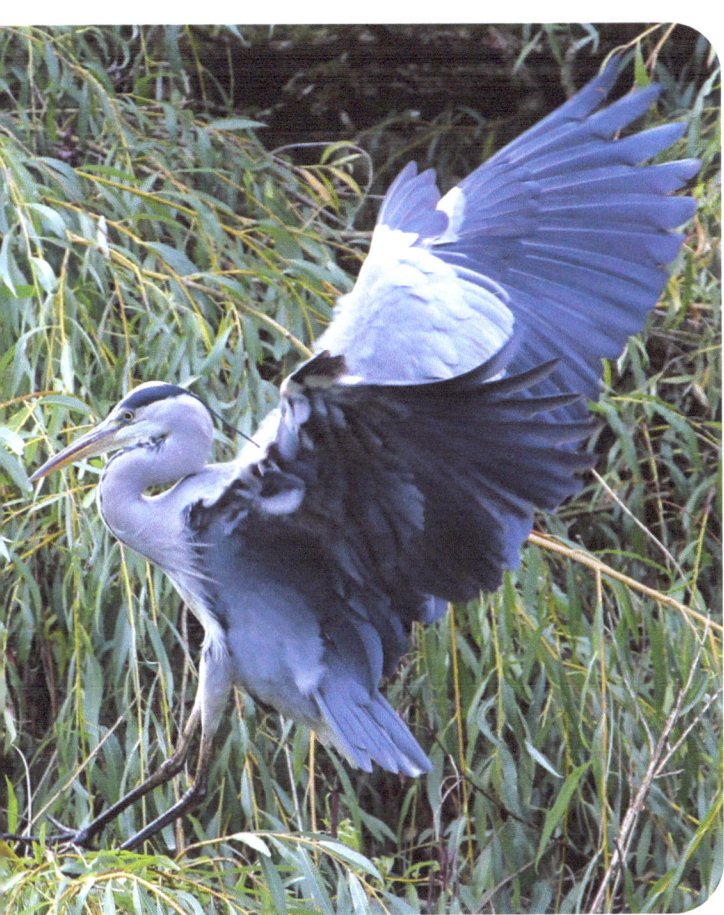

Photograph and Coloring by Jo Warren

On the next page I will walk you through the coloring of the Great Blue Heron which is on page 6 of this coloring book. The drawing was inspired by a beautiful photograph by Intricate Art Coloring Group leader, Jo Warren. She captured the Great blue heron's spectacular wings during the birds landing. Using only a few blue, gray and white colored pencils you can you can give depth, movement, and color to this amazing bird!

❯ Supply List

In this lesson I used colored pencils from the Tombow Irojiten Rainforest Dictionary Set. (pencil numbers listed below)

1) The coloring page can be found on page 6

2) Colors: (LG 3) Sallow, (P10) Pigeon Gray, (DL 7) Jay Blue, (V7) Kingfisher, (D8) Midnight Blue

3) Pencil Sharpener: An electric pencils sharpener is easy to use and works best to keep your pencils extra sharp and your hand less sore. But if you don't have one, no problem. A hand pencil sharpener works just fine too.

GRAYSCALE COLORING LESSON
Great Blue Heron

Great Blue Heron
Supplies needed: 6 colored pencils

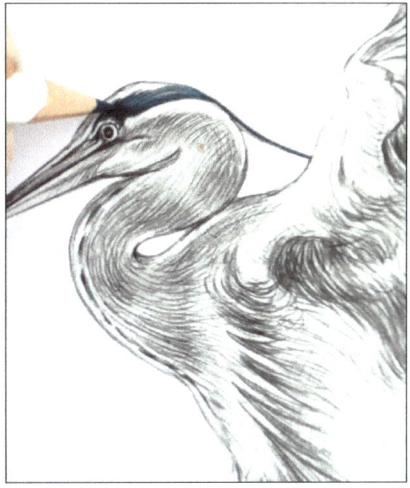

Step 1. Start by coloring in the head band on your heron using (D8) Midnight Blue. Make it nice and dark by layering the color serveral times.

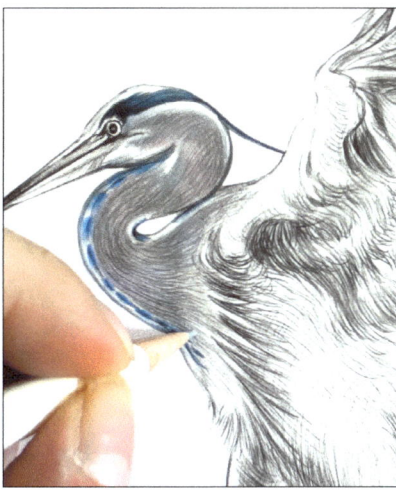

Step 2. Next color in the neck using (P10) Pigeon Gray and (DL7) Jay Blue on the spots running down the front of the neck.

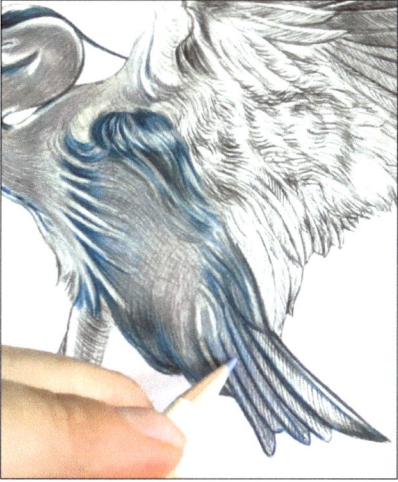

Step 3. For the heron's body first layer (P10) and then build up the blue with (DL7) and then the dark accents with (V7) Midnight Blue.

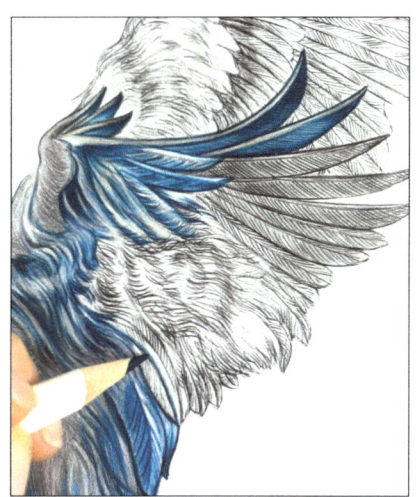

Step 4. Continue to work your way up the wings layering blues from light to dark. First (DL7) then (V7) and finally (D8).

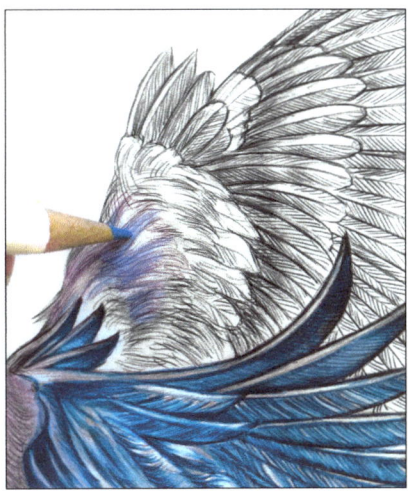

TIP. Adding lighter blues under your darker outlines will make the blues pop more.

Coloring Steps by Jo Warren

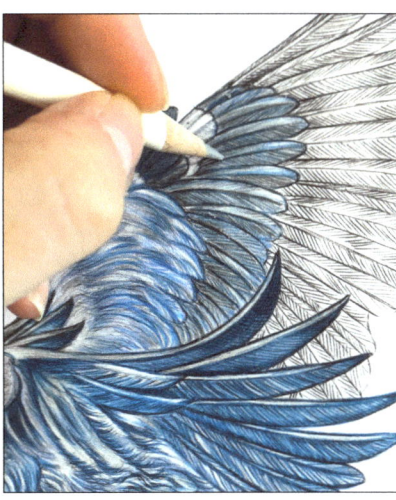

Step 5. Add gray (P10) to the top side of the feathers will make them appear to have a highlight and appear more three dimensional

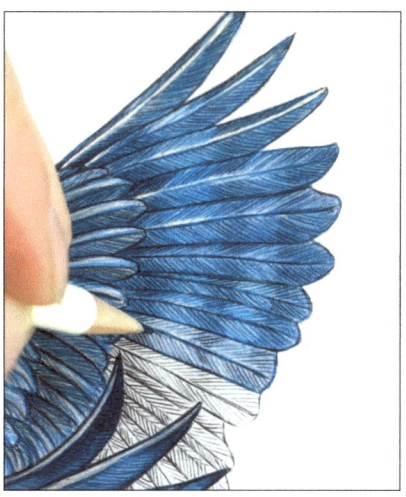

Step 6. To add detail to your piece color directly over the lines of the feathers with your darkest blue (D8).

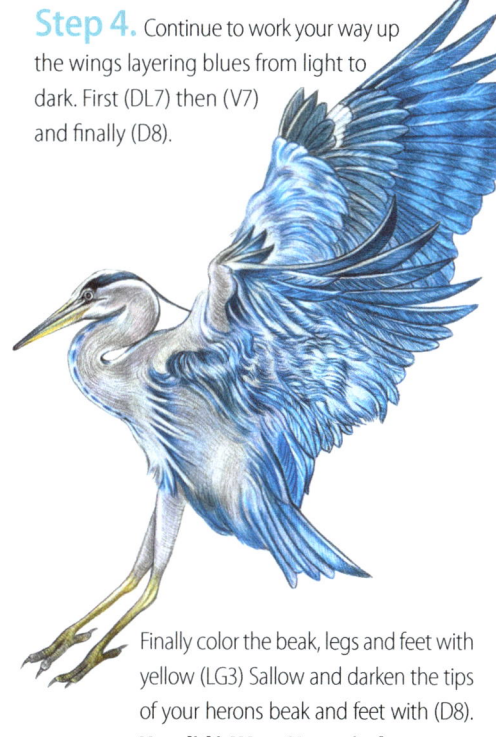

Finally color the beak, legs and feet with yellow (LG3) Sallow and darken the tips of your herons beak and feet with (D8).
You did it! Your Heron is done.

Spreading Awareness through *Coloring*

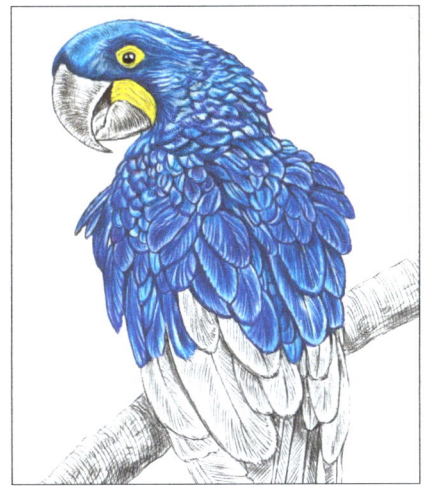

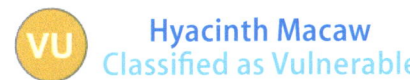
Hyacinth Macaw
Classified as Vulnerable

I truly believe that raising awareness through the sharing of my artwork is a fantastic way to educate people about conservation. And coloring animals is a beautiful way to learn about them as you enjoy a relaxing and fun pastime. On the following page I listed birds status on the *International Union for Conservation of Nature's (IUCN)* conservation list. I thought it would be important to include the *(IUCN)* conservation list so people could understand the classifications more clearly. To the right is an overview of the IUCN's conservation list, which breaks animals' conservation status into several categories. Knowing what these categories mean and the animals that are included in them is extremely important. **Together through art we can change the world!**

Tim Jeffs
Animal Artist

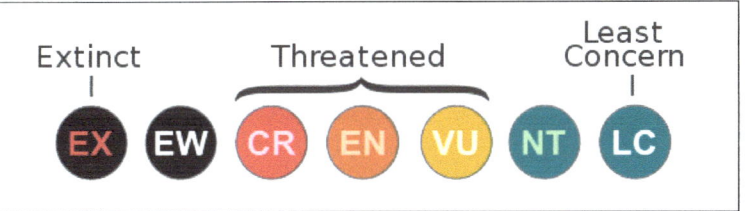

The list consists of 7 categories. From Least Concerned all the way to Extinct. Here are the definitions of each category:

- **LEAST CONCERN (LC):** A species that has been evaluated but not qualified for any other category on the list.
- **NEAR THREATENED (NT):** A species that may be considered threatened with extinction in the near future.
- **VULNERABLE (VU):** A species likely to become endangered unless the circumstances that are threatening its survival and reproduction improve.
- **ENDANGERED (EN):** A species that is considered very likely to become extinct.
- **CRITICALLY ENDANGERED (CR):** A species that is facing an extremely high risk of becoming extinct in the wild.
- **EXTINCT IN THE WILD (EW):** A species that is only known by living members kept in captivity or as a naturalized population outside its historic range due to massive habitat loss.
- **EXTINCT (EX):** A species that has been terminated.

Learn about the Birds

Before you start coloring it's important to learn where the birds in this book live and know their conservation status. Many of them are doing well and thriving and are considered least concern while a few are vulnerable or threatened.

❱ African Wood Owl
This medium-sized owl lives in Africa and It is strictly nocturnal. **Conservation Status: Least Concern**

❱ Andean Cock-of-the-Rock
Regarded as the national bird of Peru they live in the Andean cloud forests in South America.
Conservation Status: Least Concern

❱ Bateleur
Considered the national emblem of Zimbabwe this medium size eagle lives in Africa and small parts of Arabia. **Conservation Status: Near Threatened**

❱ Blue Jay
Native to eastern North America the name "jay" derives from its noisy, garrulous nature.
Conservation Status: Least Concern

❱ Budgerigar
A seed eating parrot found throughout the drier parts of Australia they are nicknamed the budgie, or in American English, the parakeet.
Conservation Status: Least Concern

❱ Great Blue Heron
Found near the shores and in wetlands in North America and Central America, as well as the Caribbean and the Galápagos Islands
Conservation Status: Least Concern

❱ Greater Bird of Paradise
The greater bird-of-paradise is distributed to lowland and hill forests of southwest New Guinea and Aru Islands, Indonesia
Conservation Status: Least Concern

❱ Green Aracari
Found in the lowland forests of northeastern South America and the amazon basin.
Conservation Status: Least Concern

❱ Himalayan Monal
Native to Himalayan forests and shrublands at elevations of 2,100–4,500 m (6,900–14,800 ft)
Conservation Status: Least Concern

❱ Hyacinth Macaw
This parrot is native to central and eastern South America. From head to the tip of its long pointed tail is about one meter (3.3 ft)
Conservation Status: Vulnerable

❱ Pesquet's Parrot (Dracula Parrot)
Found in the rainforest in New Guinea, it is also known as the Dracula parrot or vulturine parrot.
Conservation Status: Vulnerable

❱ Ruff
Breeds in marshes and wet meadows across northern Eurasia, its winter grounds include southern and western Europe, Africa, southern Asia and Australia.
Conservation Status: Least Concern

❱ Red Breasted Goose
Breeds in Arctic Siberia and winter along the north-western shores of the Black Sea in Bulgaria, Romania and Ukraine. **Conservation Status: Vulnerable**

❱ Secretary Bird
Endemic to Africa, it is usually found in the open grasslands and savanna of the sub-Saharan region.
Conservation Status: Vulnerable

❱ Sulphur-crested cockatoo
This relatively large white cockatoo is found in wooded habitats in Australia, New Guinea and some of the islands of Indonesia
Conservation Status: Least Concern

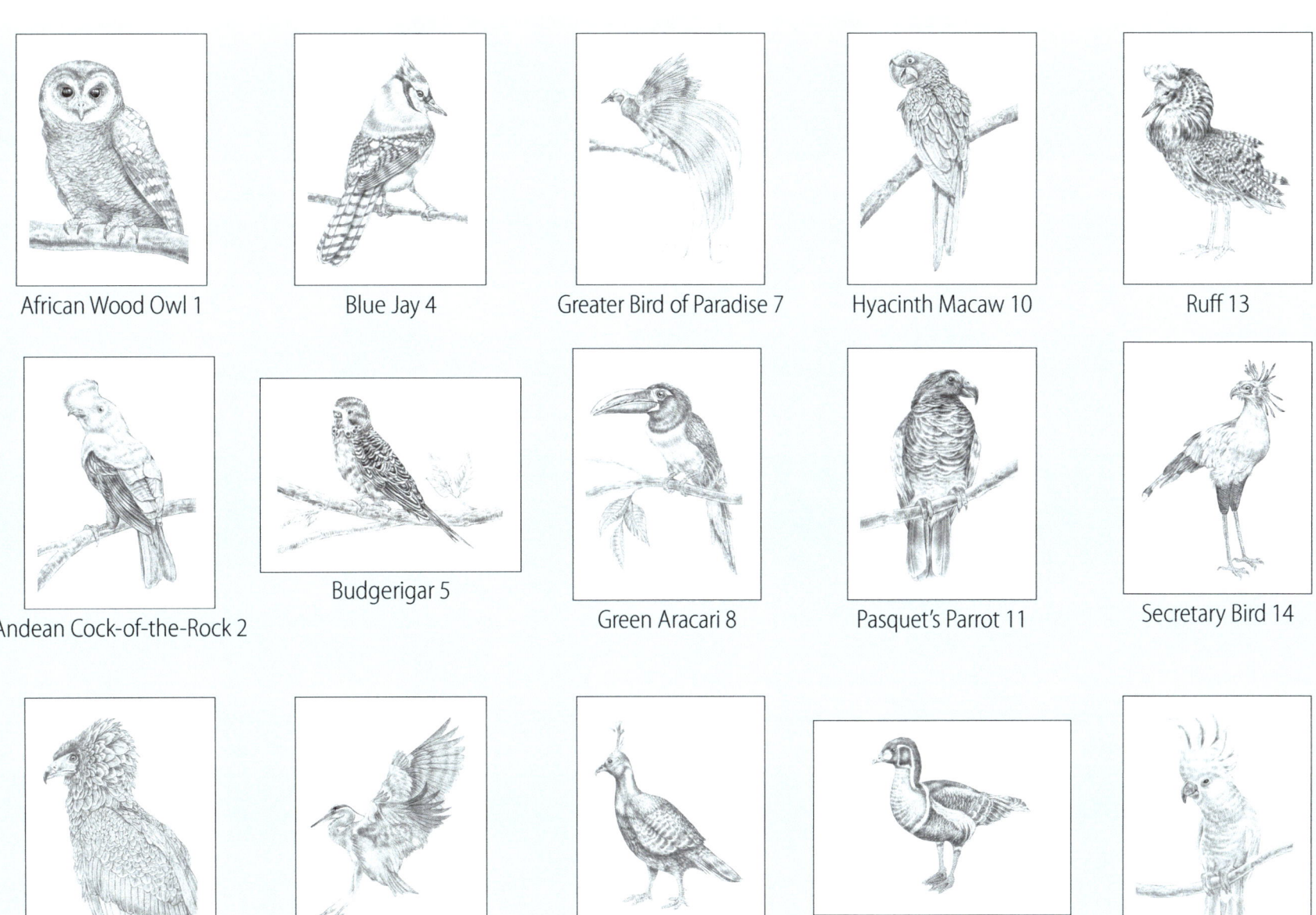

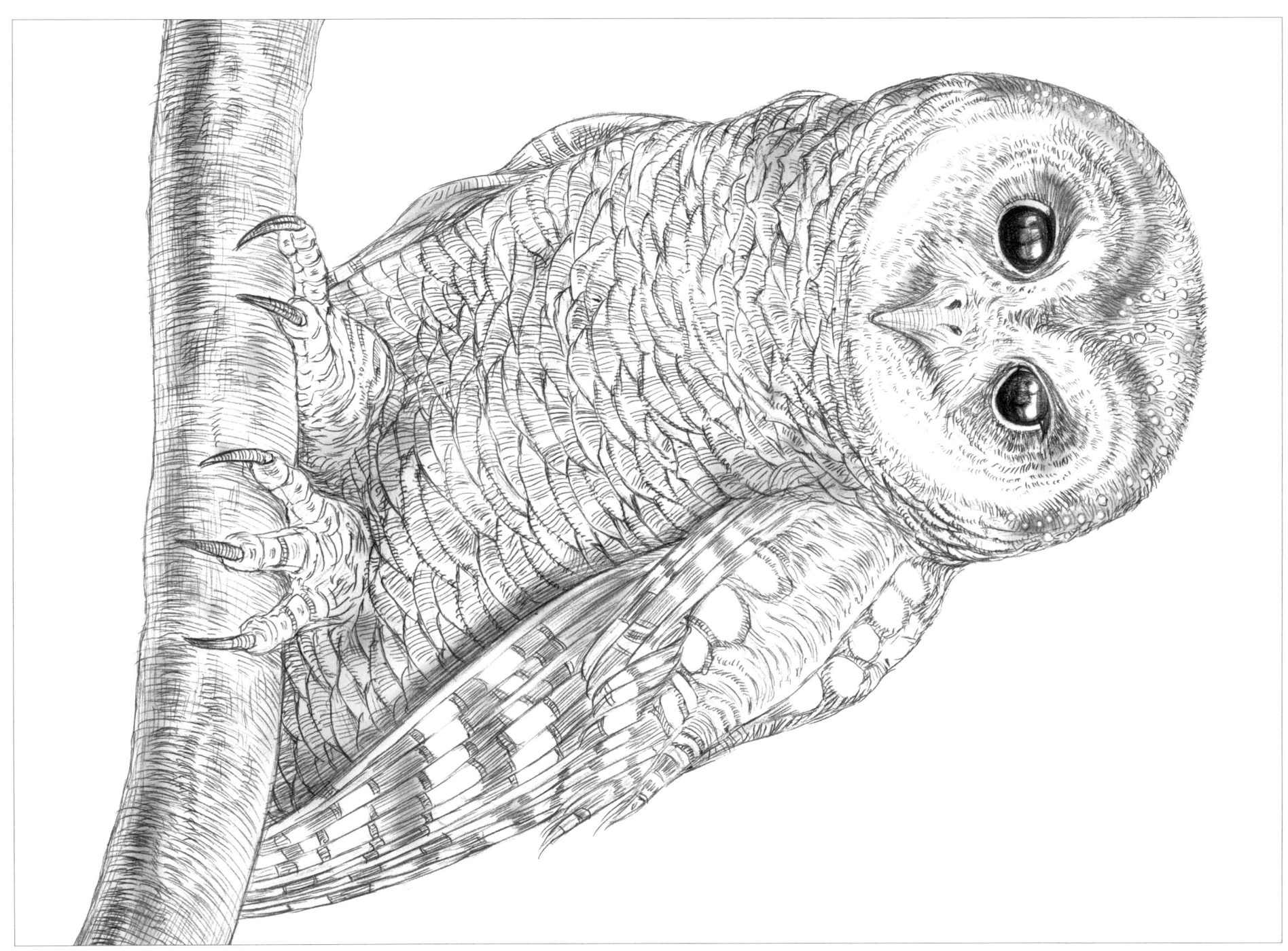

African Wood Owl

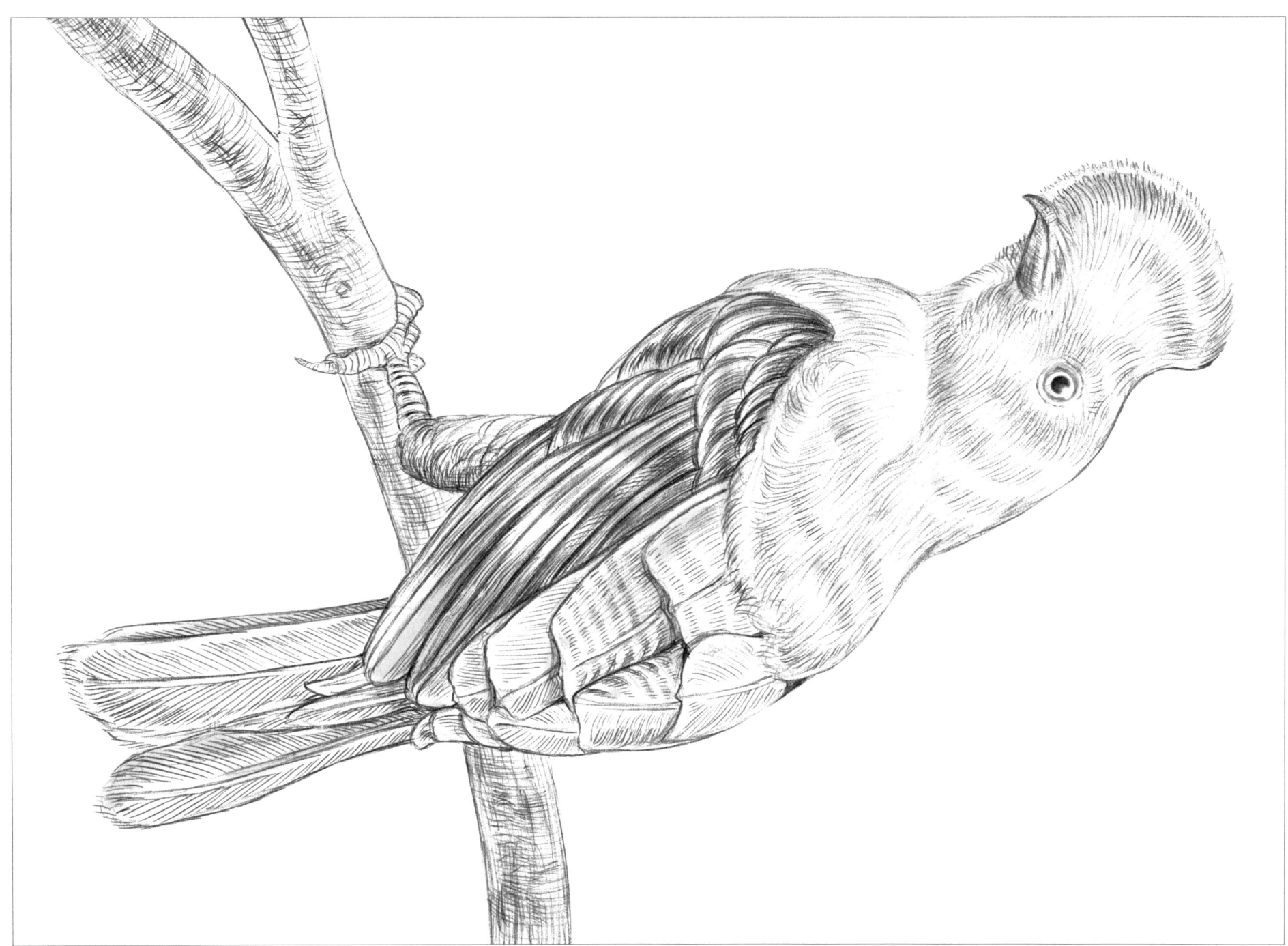

Andean Cock-of-the-Rock

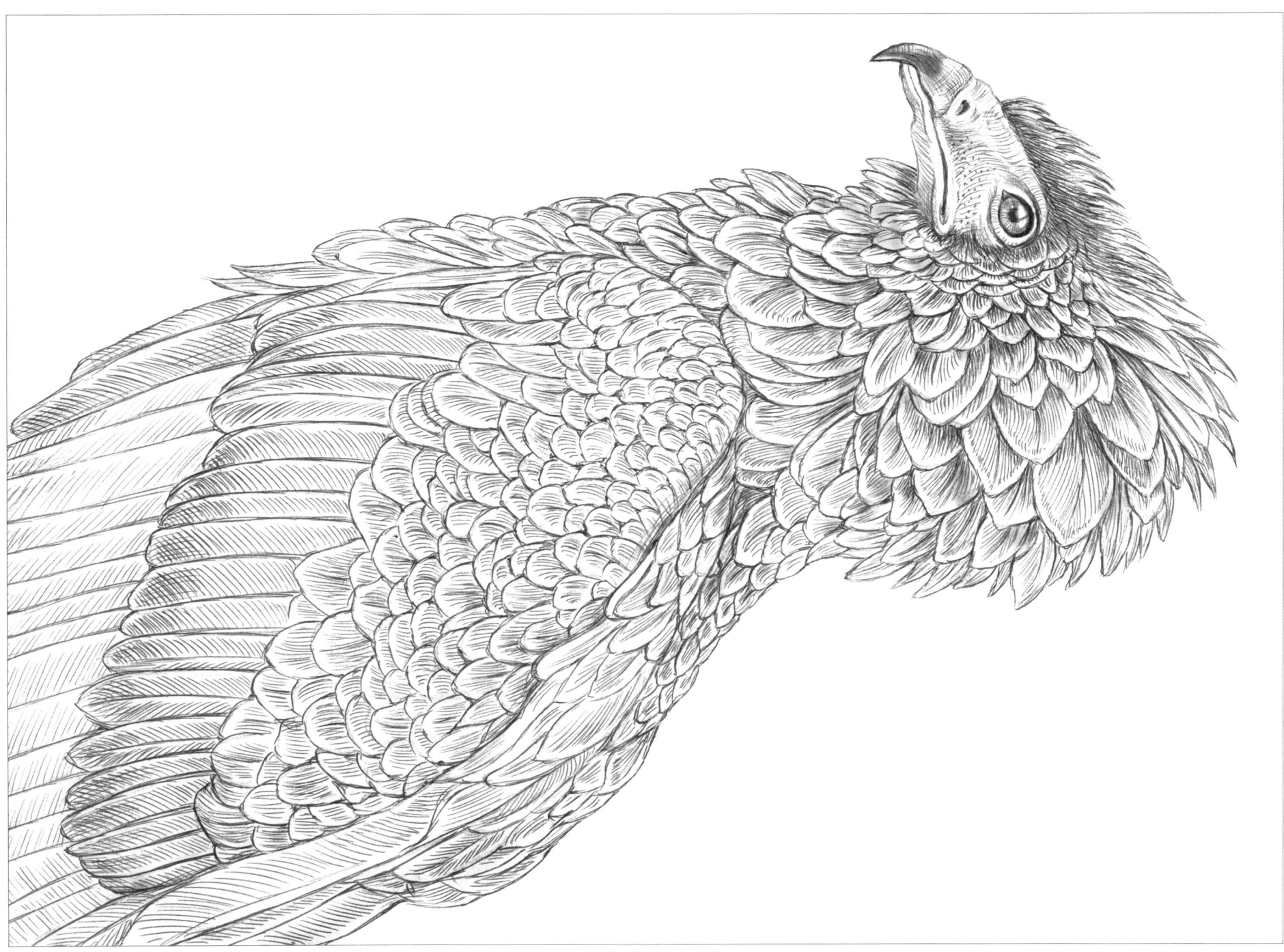

Bateleur

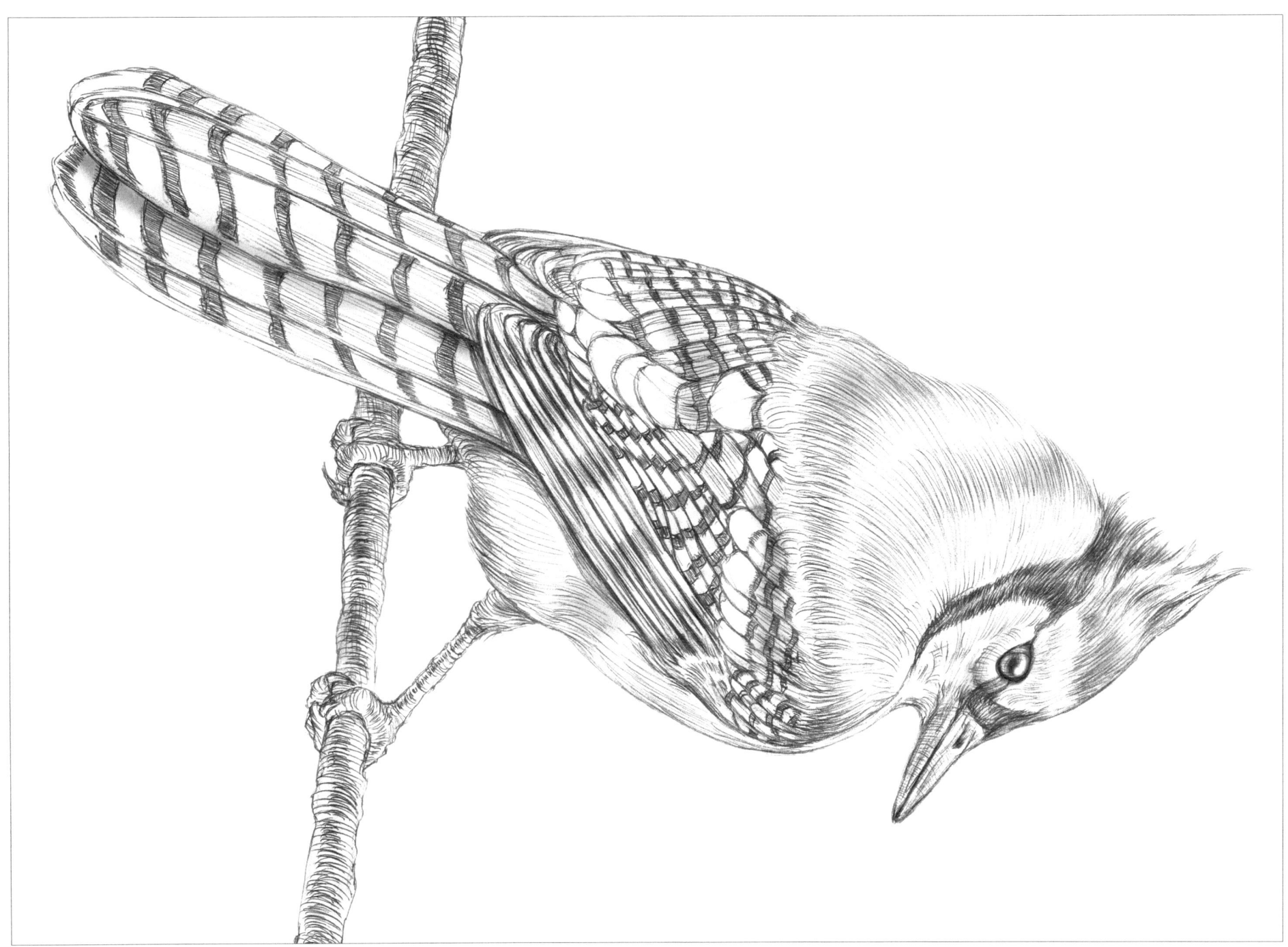

Blue Jay

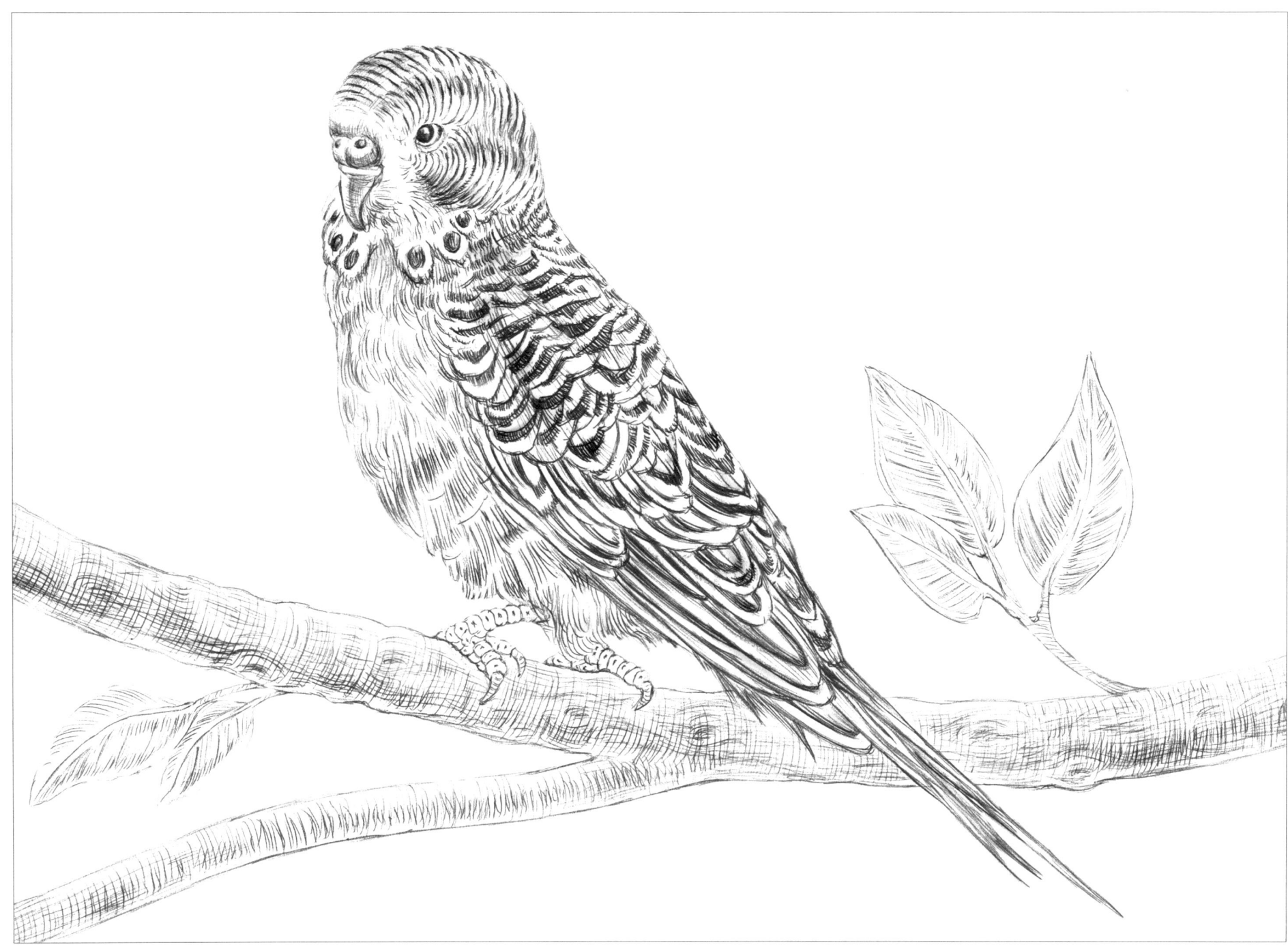

Budgerigar

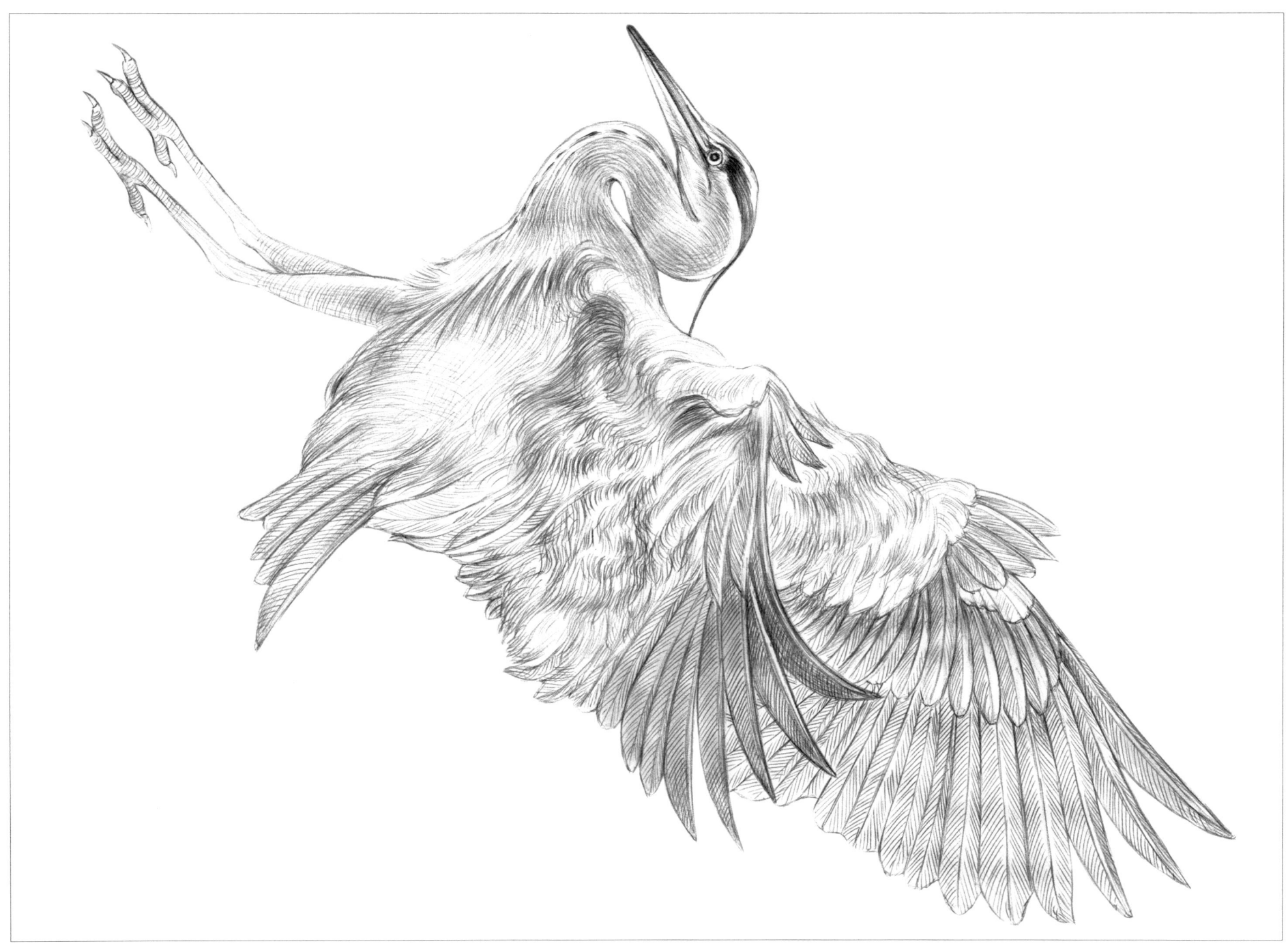

Great Blue Heron

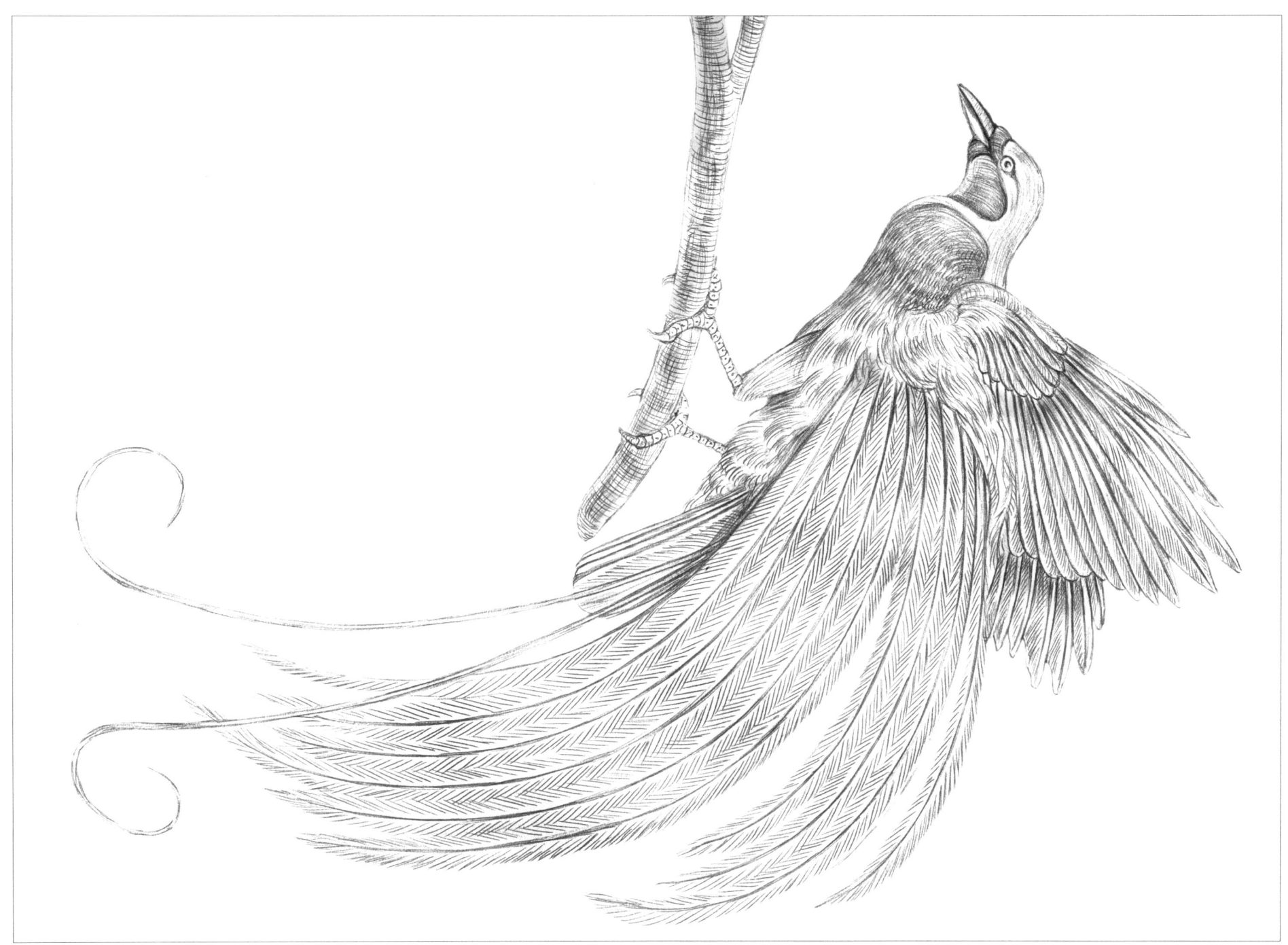

Greater Bird of Paradise

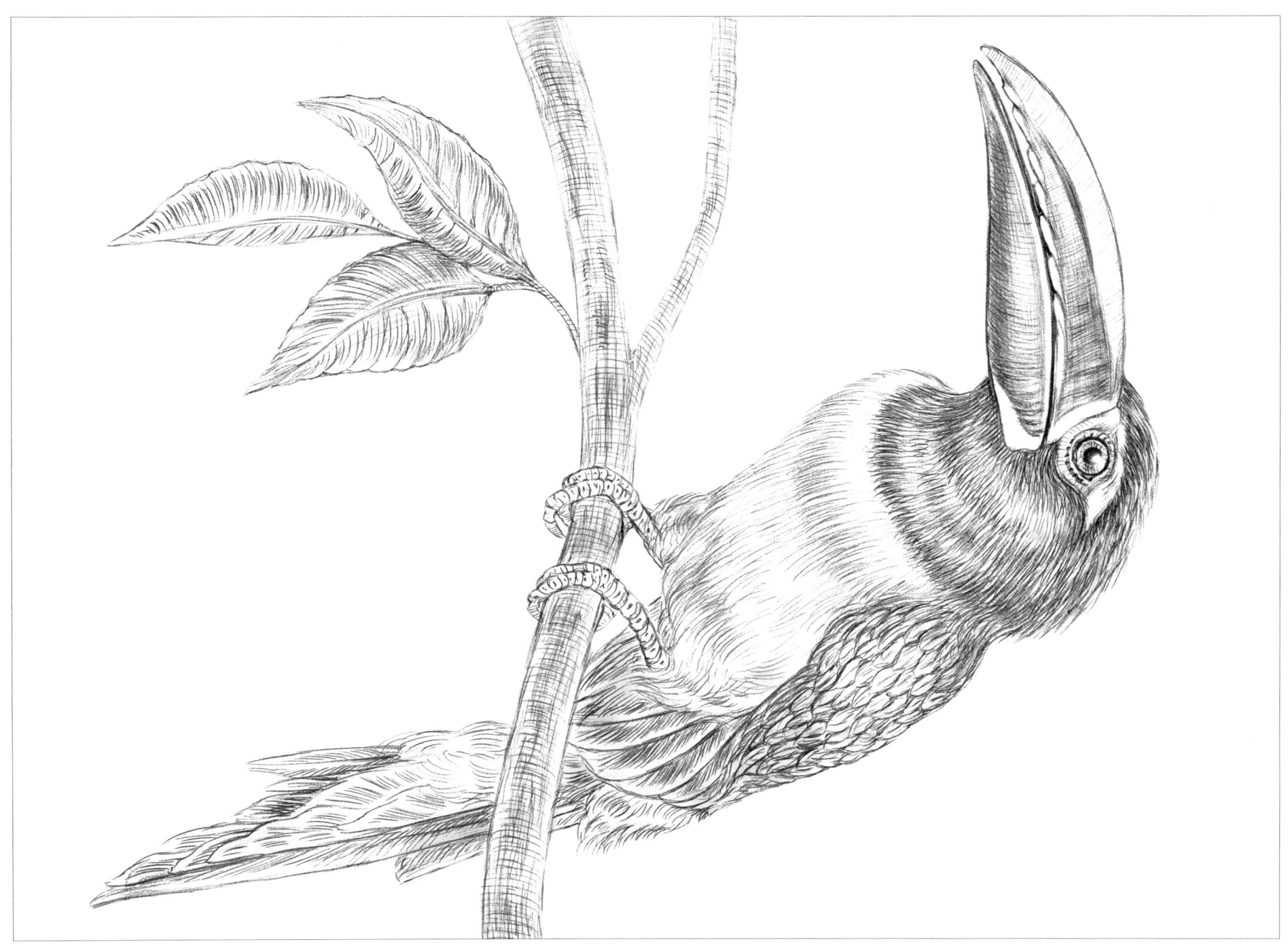

Green Aracari

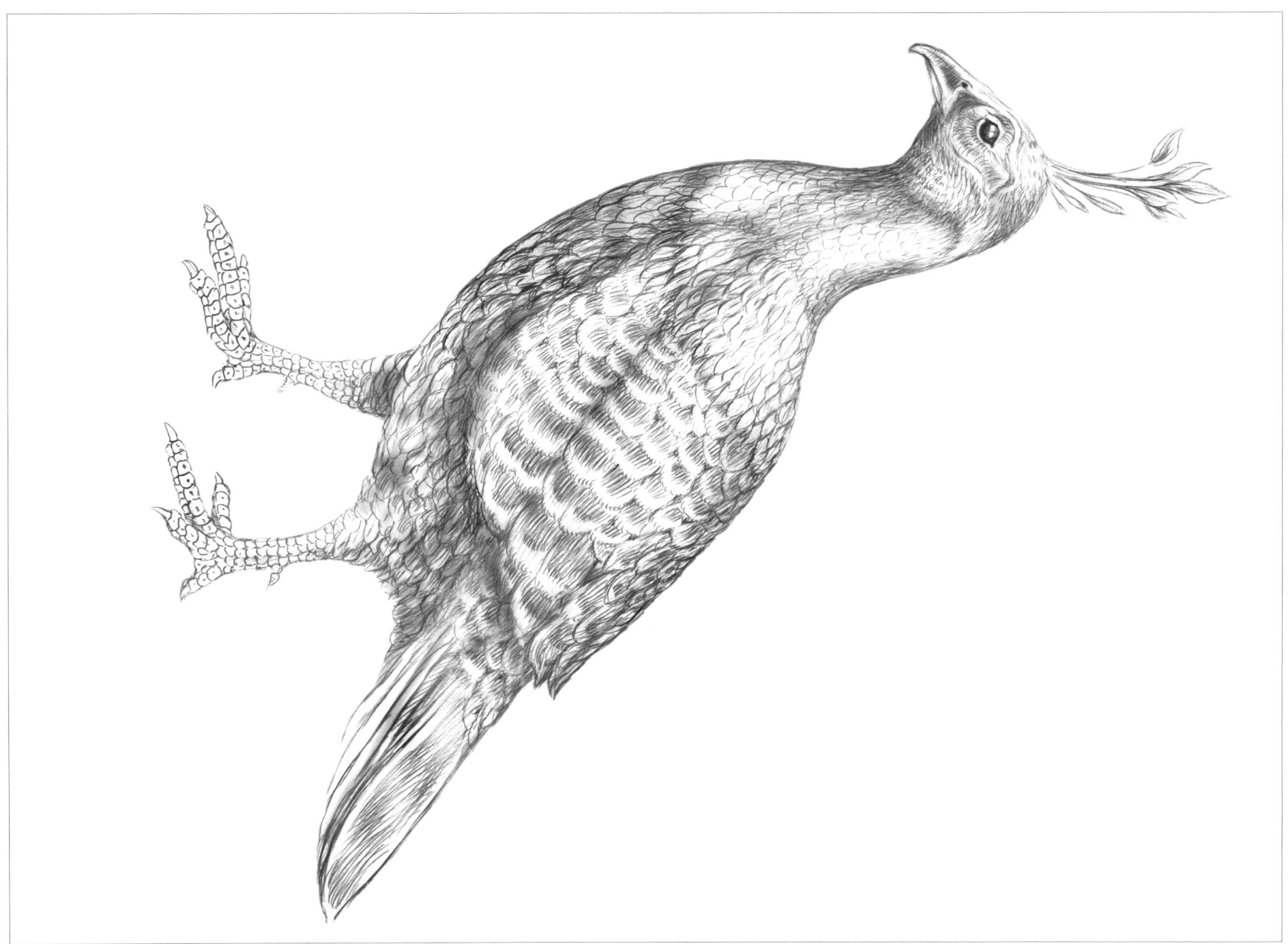

Himalayan Monal

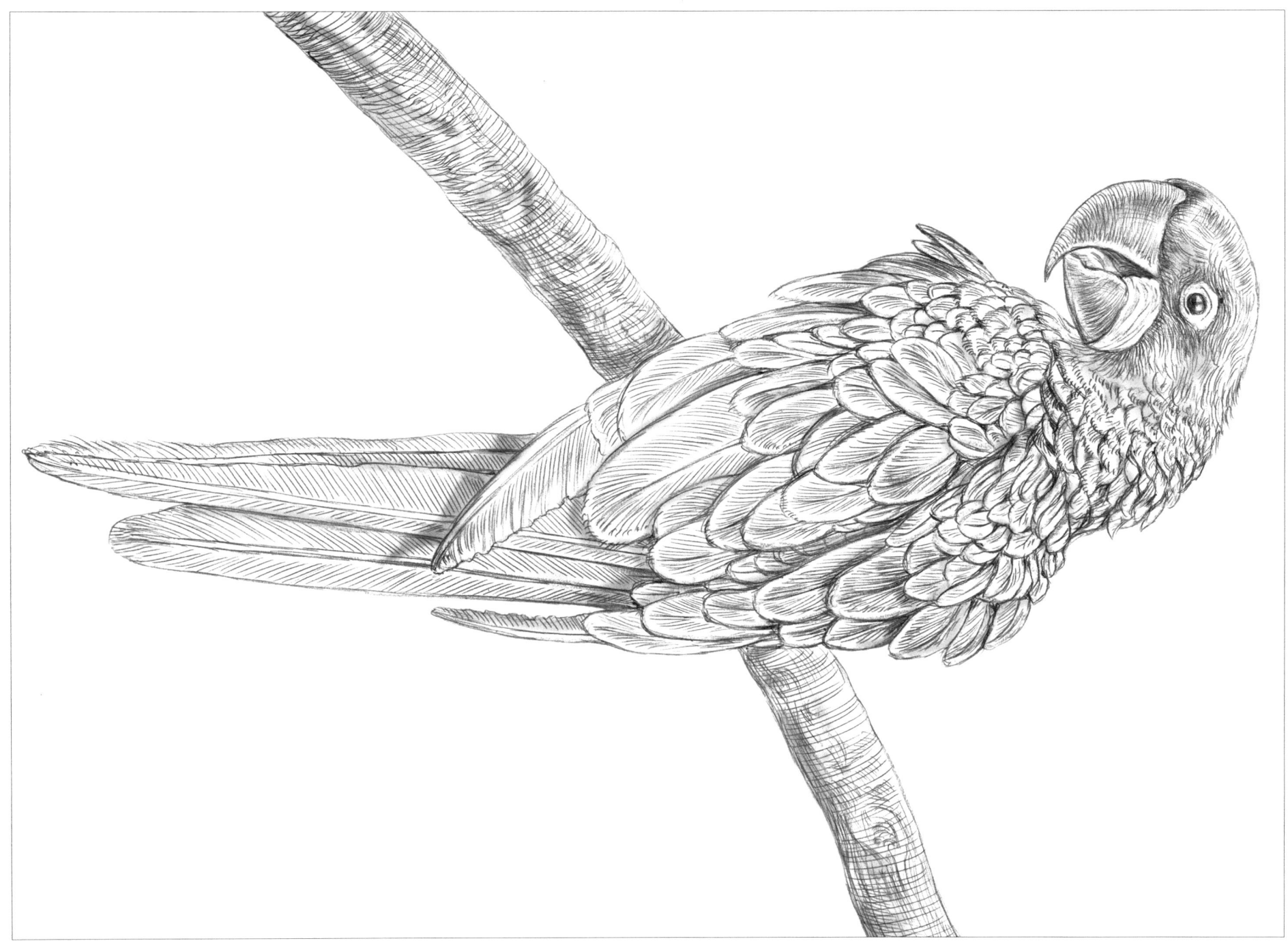

Hyacinth Macaw

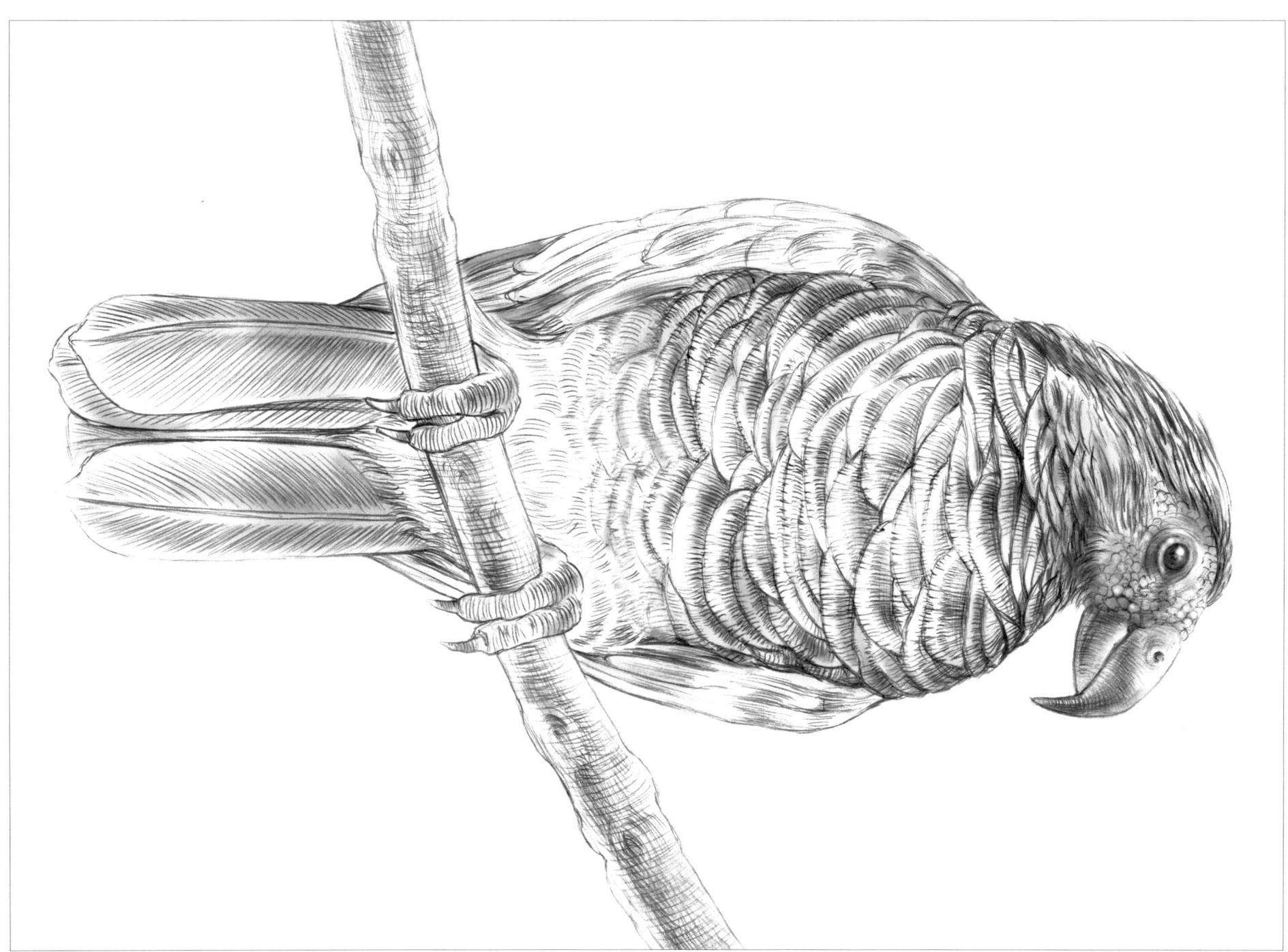

Pesquet's Parrot (Dracula Parrot)

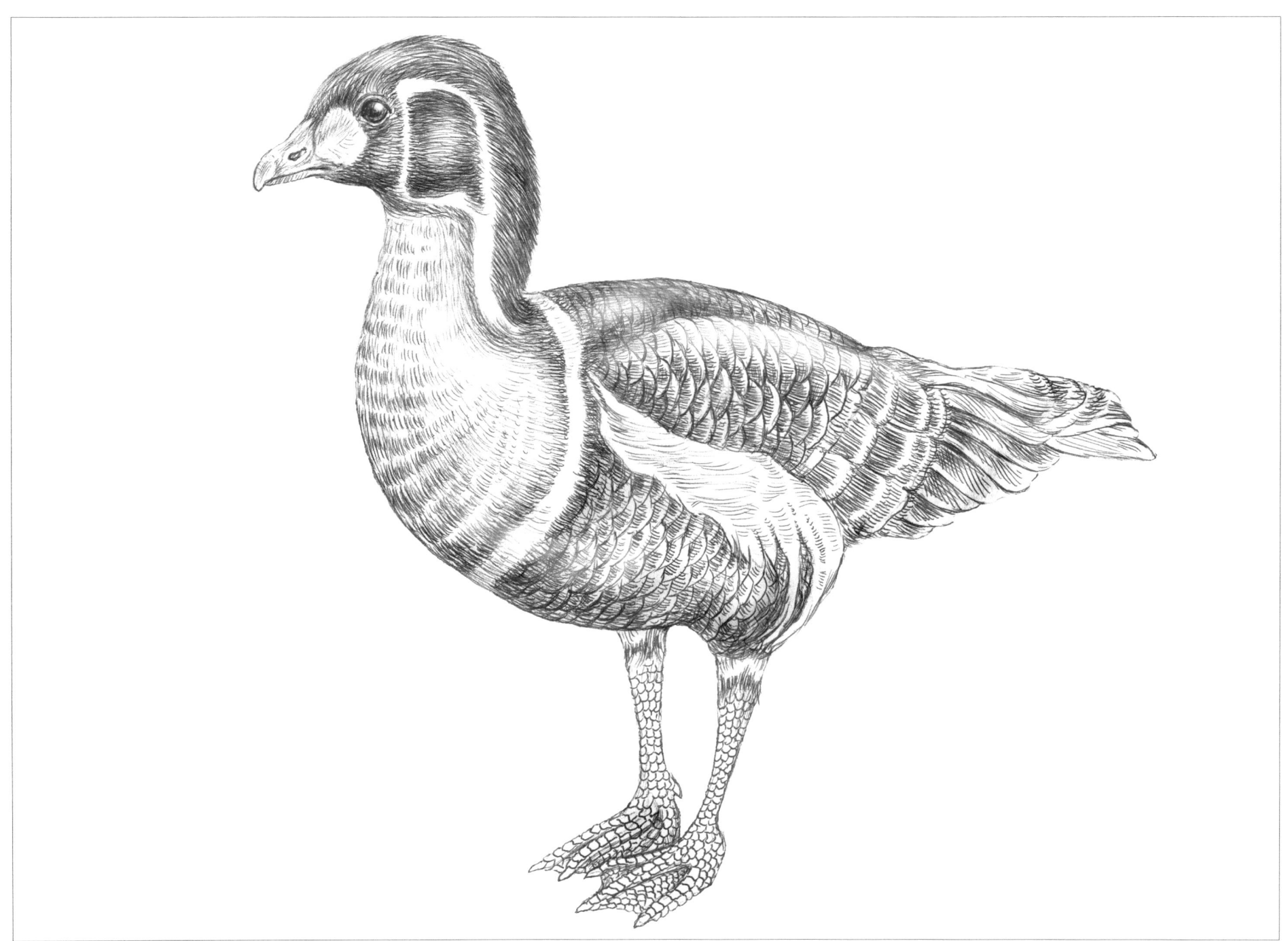

Red Breasted Goose

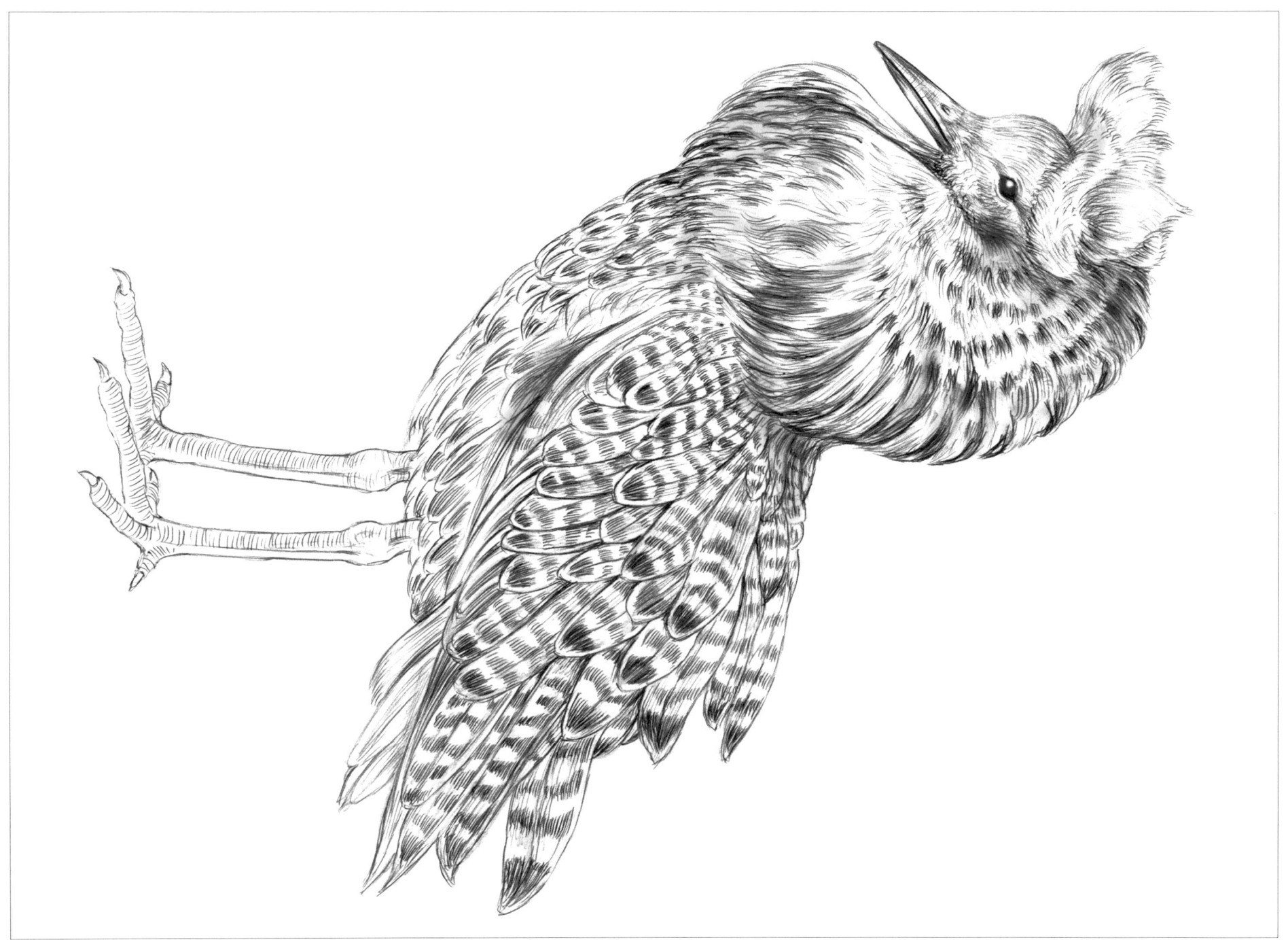

Ruff

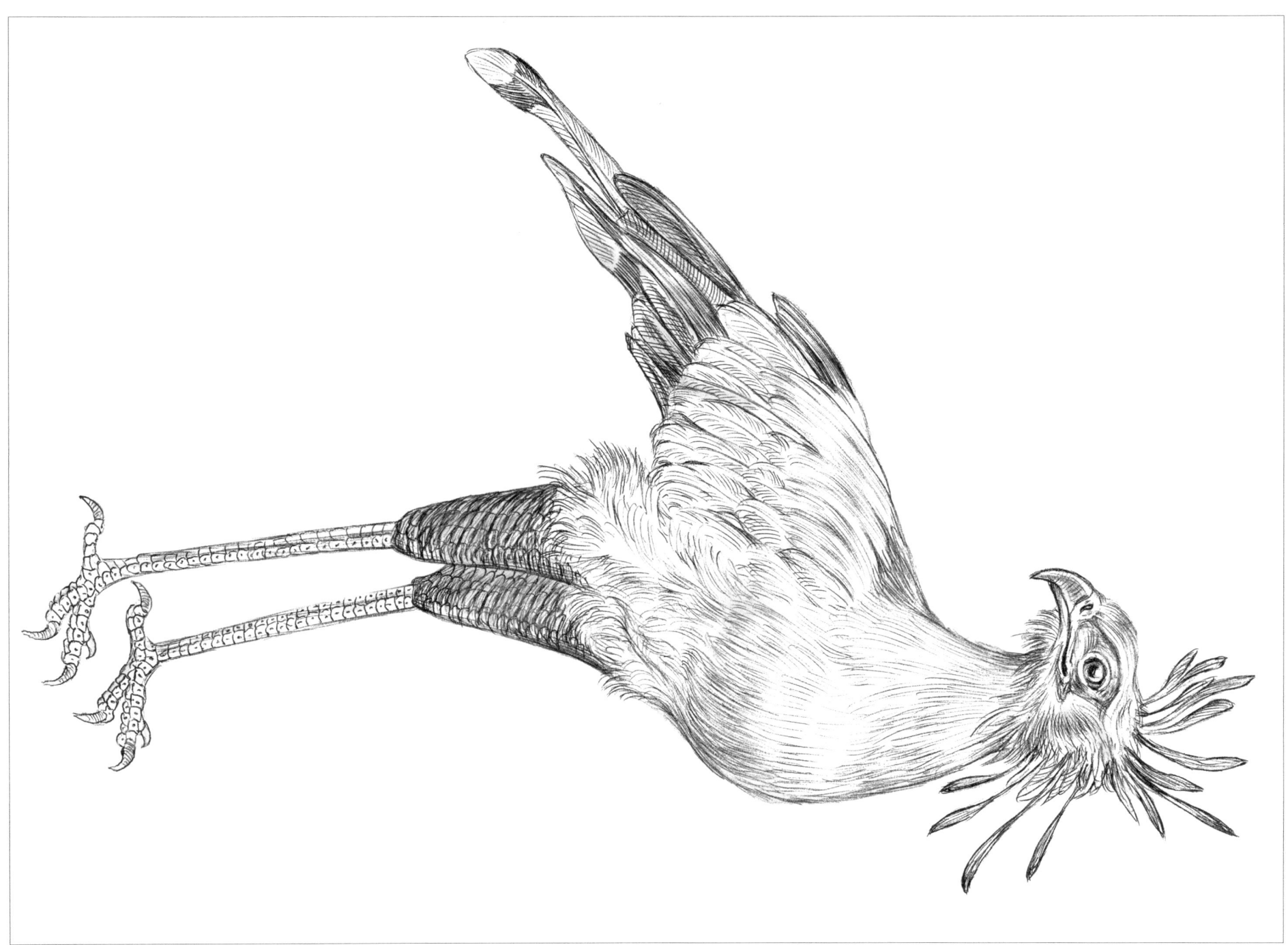

Secretary Bird

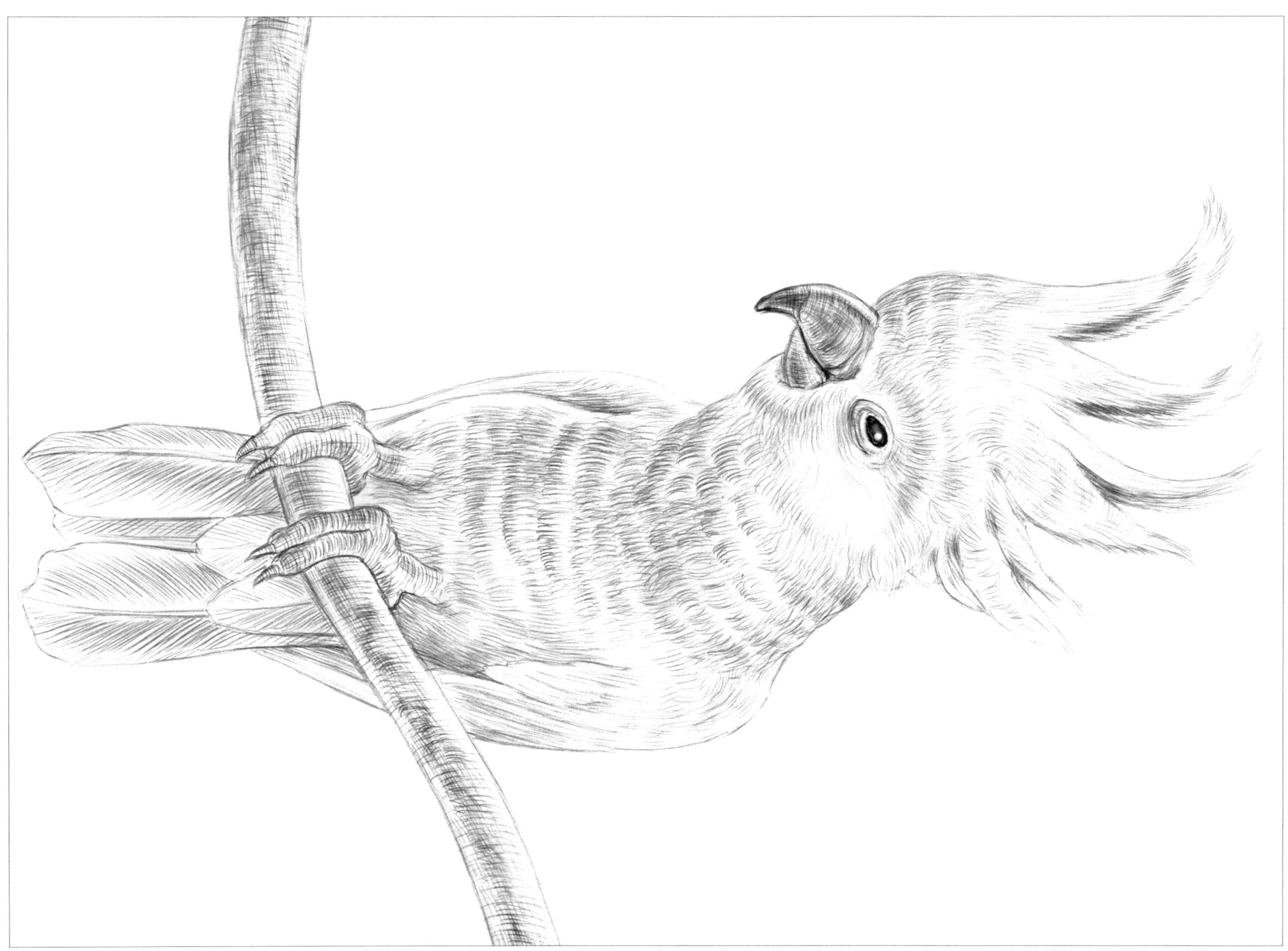

Sulphur-crested cockatoo

Tim Jeffs is a New York City based artist and illustrator who has been creating dynamic artwork for over 25 years. Animals are a favorite subject matter of his, along with the complex and intricate details these creatures possess. *"The incredible diversity and complexity of animals has always intrigued me. They offer endless pleasure to look and marvel upon. In every drawing I try to capture the unique quality of each particular animal. I hope you enjoy my perspective, love and admiration of these incredible creatures."*

Visit my website for prints, digital coloring books and coloring lessons:

www.TimJeffsArt.com

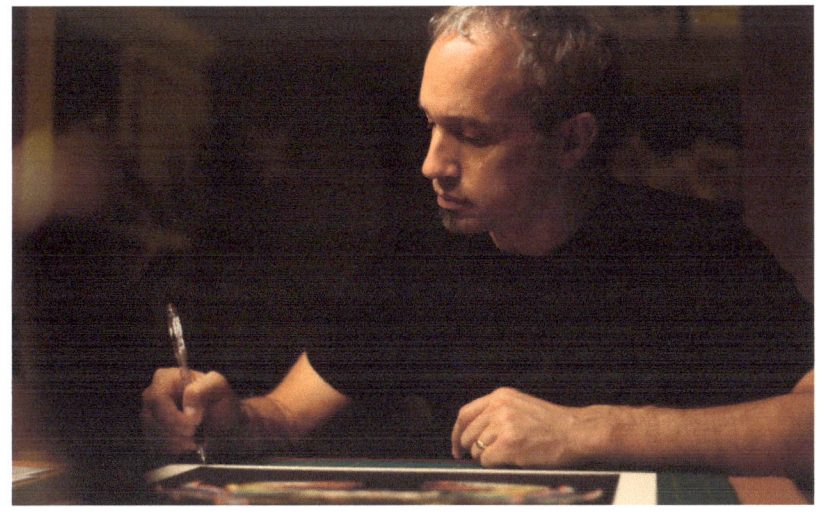

Discover the full line of Tim Jeffs' Published Coloring Books

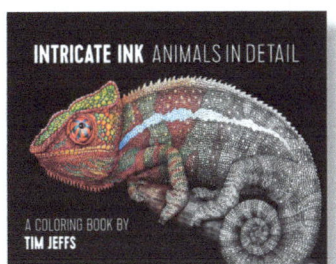 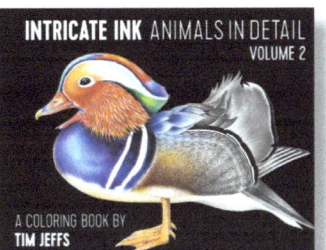 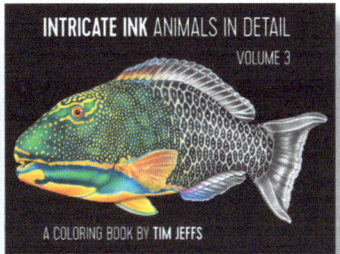 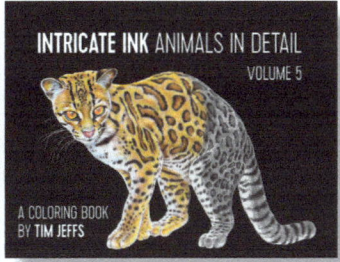 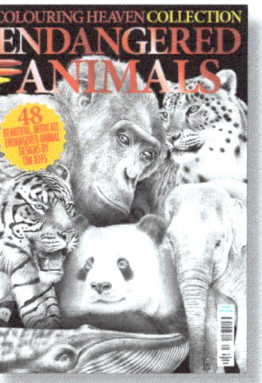

Intricate Ink Animals In Detail Volume 1, 2 3 and 5 Available at:
Pomegranate.com
Amazon.com
Bookdepository.com

**Colouring Heaven Collection
Endangered Animals**
Available at: Colouringheaven.com

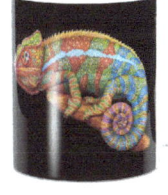

Discover Tim Jeffs' Merchandise

Etsy Shop
www.etsy.com/shop/TimJeffsArt

Society6 Shop
www.society6.com/TimJeffsArt

Redbubble Shop
TimJeffsArt.redbubble.com

Vsual Print Shop
https://vsual.co/shop/tim-jeffs-art

Discover the full line of Tim Jeffs Digital Coloring Books at:
www.TimJeffsArt.com

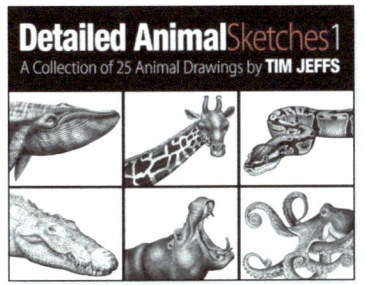 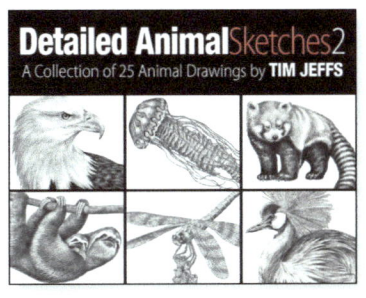 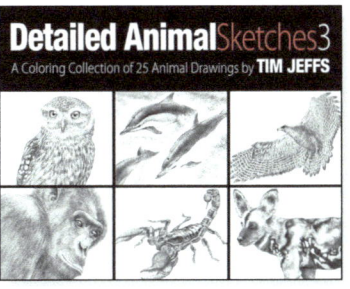 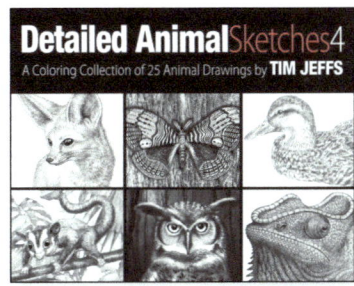 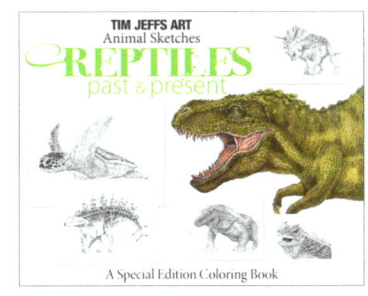

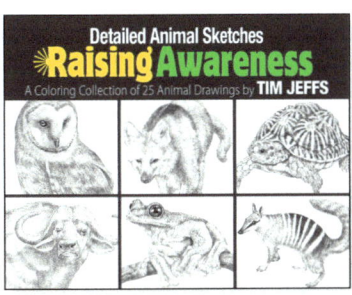 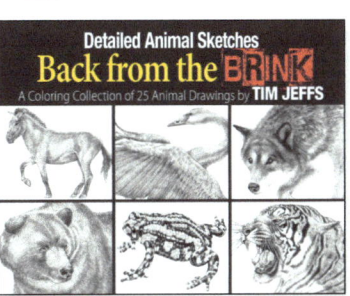 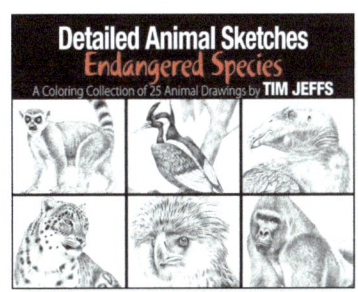 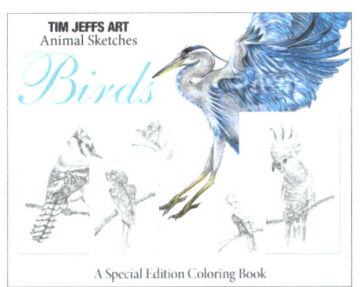 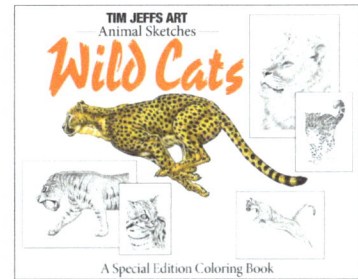

And Coloring Lessons

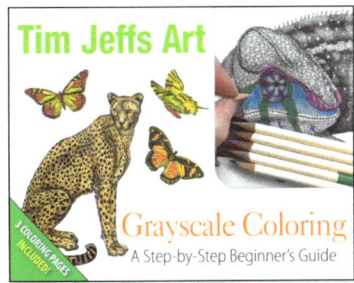 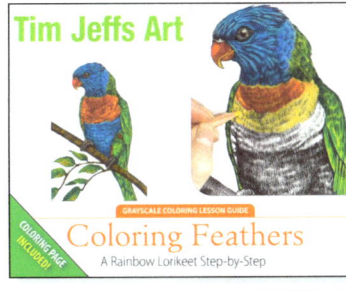 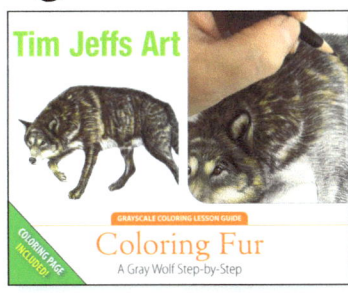 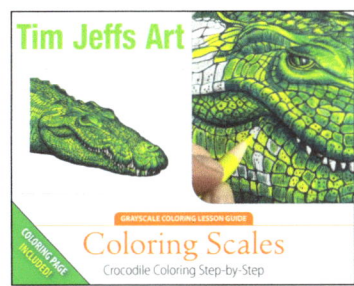 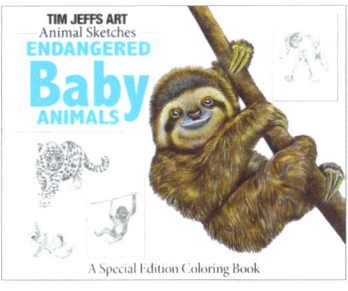

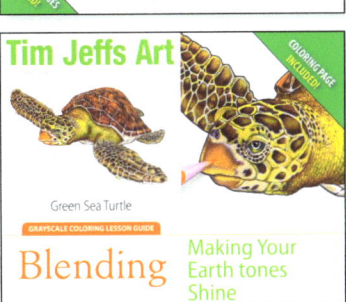 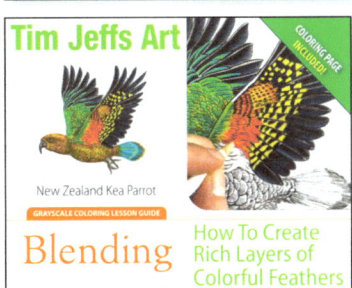 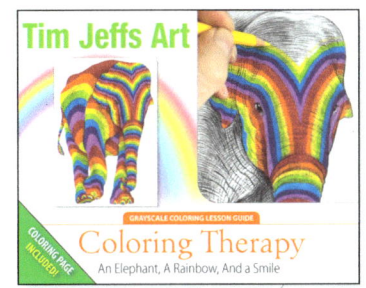 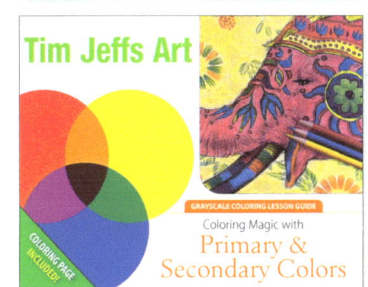 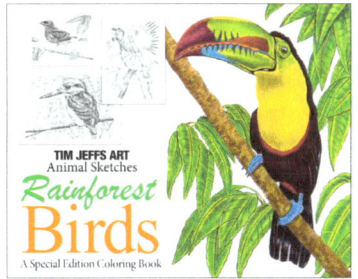

TIM JEFFS ART Online Resources

Share Your Creativity with the World!

Join the ever-expanding coloring group of animal lovers who inspire each other through their colorings of the animals from Tim's books and lessons. With thousands of members from all around the world, Tim's Facebook group "Intricate Ink Coloring Group" is a creative and safe space where everyone is welcome. Jo Warren, the groups all-inspiring administrator will welcome you in with open arms and is there to encourage everyone to just have fun no matter your coloring skill level. Come join, we can't wait to have you as a member! Join Tim's Facebook Coloring Group at:

www.facebook.com/groups/intricateink

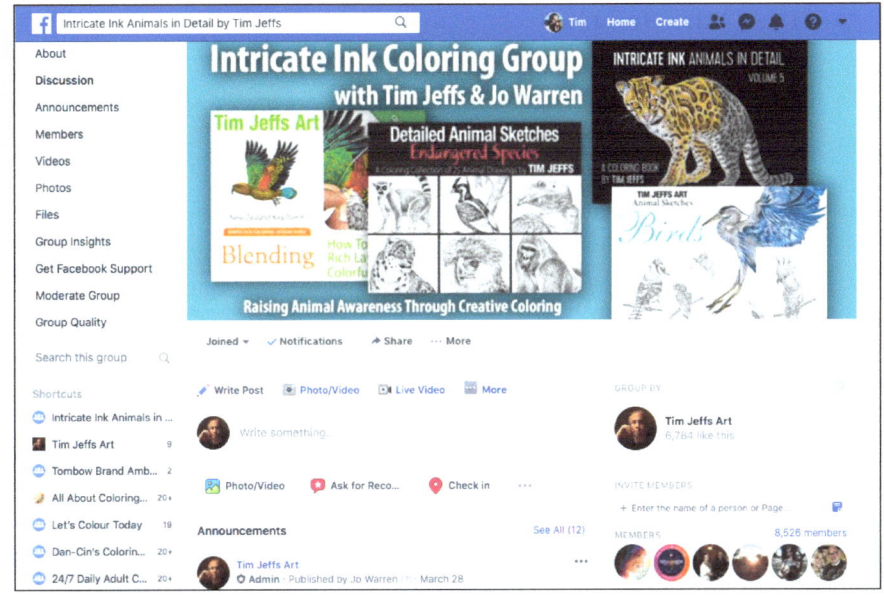

Visit the Home of Tim Jeffs Art

TimJeffsArt.com is my home on the web where I display all of my work and various projects. I hope you can stop by for a visit! You'll find my new shop where signed and unsigned prints of all of my animal drawings are available to purchase, along with the complete library of my digital download coloring books and grayscale coloring lessons. In the conservation section, you can see the projects that I am very proud of. Using my art to preserve wildlife is so important to me.

www.TimJeffsArt.com

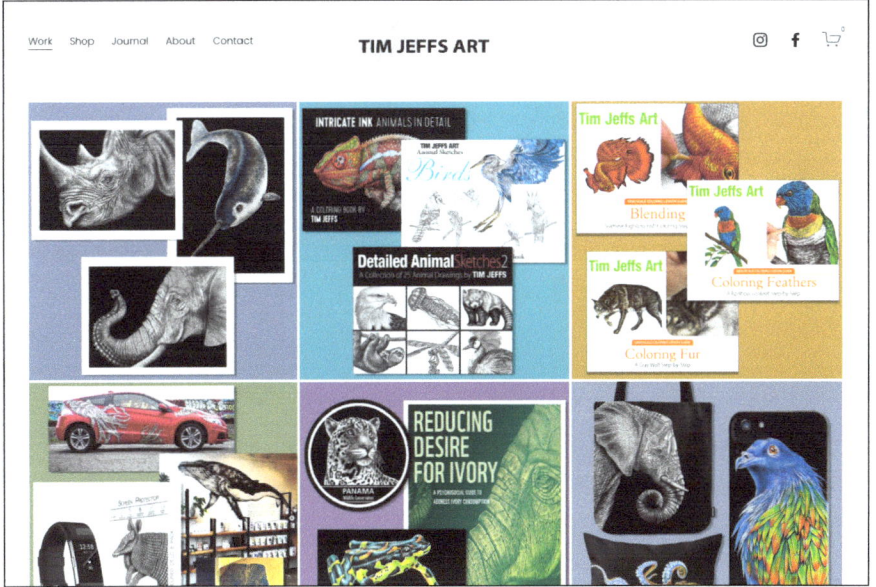